I0164605

Changing the Narrative Publishing focuses on inspirational and educational books with an emphasis on lesser heard voices. We believe that there are many stories that contribute to the landscape of culture and all voices deserve to be heard.

Changing the Narrative Books

CTNBooks.com

Copyright © CTN Publishers 2020

ISBN: 978-0-9863661-4-7

Table of Contents

Foreword

Contributers

FOREWORD

This book is written in real time- the raw voices of social media recorded from the hearts of people as they watch the pandemic unfold on their screens. These words are spoken by those living through essential shortages, protesting in the streets, praying over the future of their children, nursing ailing loved ones suffering with COVID-19.

The collective groanings of America and the World have been heard across the news, the streets, and the world wide web. The writings in this book are an extension of the emotions that many navigate as the anxieties of a pandemic converge with the falling status quo of cultural and systemic racism. Several months deep into the pandemic the word 'viral' induces fear and uncertainty about public health as we do everything humanly possible to contain the spread of the novel coronavirus. However, in the context of social media the word 'viral' is something to which internet users and social media influencers aspire. To go viral means that what you have put onto the world wide web is taking the world by storm. If nothing else the events of 2020 have spread through the world like wildfire- working their way through every human- pushing us to take account of our lives and our collective future.

As you read this collection of writings from everyday people, my hope is you become infected with the truths they have chosen to share. I hope you are infected fully enough to fight for health, fight for peace, fight for change.

With Hope,

Niambi LeeKong McLaurin, Editor

Black Mother Warfare

by Niambi LeeKong McLaurin

Between coffee and
breakfast and cleaning the kitchen
Nursing my baby
I shed a few tears for George and Ahmaud
We put on our masks and run errands
The weather is beautiful
I push the baby in the stroller
As I follow my boys on their bikes I wave at the
neighbors and the mail lady-and wave away a passing
thought about what they post on their timelines
We wash our hands
And sanitize the knobs
And I cry that they will always be looked at as black
boys and not just boys
One day they will be black men and not simply men
We update the family calendar
And I write Juneteenth
Vowing again to celebrate this year
And I shed a tear
It's warfare loving yourself when the world says you
are undeserving of love
We nap and play in the yard
Video games and TV
I cook again
We eat

And talk about the anger and confusion on the news
I wonder if I'm equipping them or simply wounding
my children before the world can
We are intentional
beautiful black family
It's warfare to bloom
in a place intended for trampling feet
We take baths and read and pray
Extra kisses
Please stay longer mommy
It's warfare to make a home in the midst of a world
that wants you to live in a box
I write a little
Catch up on my shows
Kiss my husband

It's warfare
Keeping the peace in times of war

And now the whole world knows that our fears are real.

They have always been real.

Covid-19
Shelley Tyler Smith

Covid-19
is
racist too...

Still Strange Fruit
by E.E. Pritchett

I am
Uneasy
            Unsettled
Breath   less

Waiting for the next,

Not another?
death   to be played on loop

Like black bodies
Hanging
Warned to
Stay in
Your
Place

I wonder
is it not conspiracy? Complicity?
this network show and tell and show again the many
ways to take a black life

Kill the one and
traumatize
The rest

Untitled Rashaad Kareem

I can breathe
And believe we all the same
So I step forth
With no remorse
And breathe in George Floyd's name
And all you have slain
I consider it my responsibility
To stand for my people and ensure they feel free
Stemming from an American history
Choking me
And having me hung
Now you attacking my capacity
By the neck and by the lung
But you still ain't won
I can breathe
You can attack me physically
But mentally
I see who I'm meant to be
This ain't the sixties
And you're not repeating history
Right now it stops
Fuck you
And fuck your cops
Fuck your media especially Fox

Trained to put your knee on my neck
But watch my people resurrect
I understand why you try to degrade us
We come back stronger fueling your need to hate us
I can breathe
I make it my drive
consider it my destiny
until I rest in peace
To make you regret you kept me alive
So I expect your genocide
But still
I can breathe

Neglect Creates Chaos
Danielle Gilmore

The consumed yet unseen have risen while the statues
of yore
fall flat on faces that history has sold as martyrs
For too many centuries we've been
devoured with little regard
Executed with immunity
Labeled disposable and tragically deprived
Be more Martin than Malcolm has split camps that
must face the
ultimate truth that blind whiteness values neither as
human
Let it all burn
Sometimes harvesters set fire to crops in
anticipation
Of reaping
Better from what's been sowed

An American Horror

Robertson Greene

You took us across the ocean
Some of us were tossed in the sea
You said it was the land of the fertile
Free and brave to everyone but me
It's an American horror
 An American horror
The gruesome of the whips and chains
 An American horror
Forced to plow the fields of the land
 It's an American horror
 An American horror
We're dangling dead from the trees
 An American horror
Has never been kind to me
White man beats me at any given notion
Shoots me
Police me
When I've done nothing
I'm afraid to be seen in public
Because Trayvon or George could be me
 It's an American horror
 An American horror
I should have jumped in the sea
 An American horror
It's no heaven here for me
 It's an American horror
 An American horror
With your knees pressing on my wind
 An American horror
Get off me mister
I can't breathe

White Privilege

Holly Chesnut

I want to rage.
I want to break glass
Set fires
that burn red and yellow and orange
I want to spray paint black words
on a white background,
words that inspire change.
I want to chant "say her name!"
til I'm blue in the face
so loudly,
so often,
that they do what I am demanding.

But I don't.
I am afraid.
Not of the protestors, but of the police.

I want to embrace, defend, and support
my Black friends,
their families
my Black students.
Protect them.
Stand up for them.
Prove that their lives matter

But I can't
just worry
about the Black people I know.
And neither can you.
This is bigger than that.

16

I want my rage to infiltrate
every corner of this country
But I'll start here.
where I come from, some people
still use the N-word.
They glare at my
Black Lives Matter and
Bernie and
Resist t-shirts.
I glare back
at their Confederate flags and MAGA hats.

I should've raged
when the police
asked me if I was okay
When I was parked with my black boyfriend.

I should've raged
When the gas station around the corner
Made their pumps prepaid only
Just for the week of
My Historically Black University's homecoming.

I should've raged
when the police merely laughed at my
words of disrespect
I was going 80 in a 55
But he made me late for work
I left with only a ticket

I should've raged
when my stepfather's cop friend
Jokingly told me he'd arrest me
So I would miss my flight to Hawaii

I naively told him that he couldn't arrest me
Because I hadn't done anything illegal.
He smirked and said that didn't matter.

I want to rage.
I want to expose white privilege,
including my own.
I want to repent
for all the times I used it
knowingly and unknowingly
I want to see justice, peace, and real change
Evolve from something
Black people have been demanding for generations.
I want to chastise every prosecutor and judge
that won't go after
cops who murder
innocent Black men, women, and
children.

I want to rage at myself
for being complacent
for too long

White privilege allows white people
to never think about race.
Ever.
It doesn't even occur to some of us
until we hear "Black Lives Matter."
And then the responses are
"All lives matter"
and
"Blue lives matter"
These misguided white people
still don't get it.

How can they still not get it?

So I wear my t-shirts around town
and try to be an example.
I confront my Trump-voting
MAGA hat-wearing relatives
And make sure that my vote
Cancels out at least one of theirs
In every election.

And I rage.
And I pray.

It's not enough.
I feel powerless.
But do I have the right to feel that way?
Because the irony is,
it is white privilege
that allows me the option
to speak on this,
or to remain silent,
to describe how this moment,
how this movement feels to me
or to ignore it altogether.

But I rage.
And I pray.

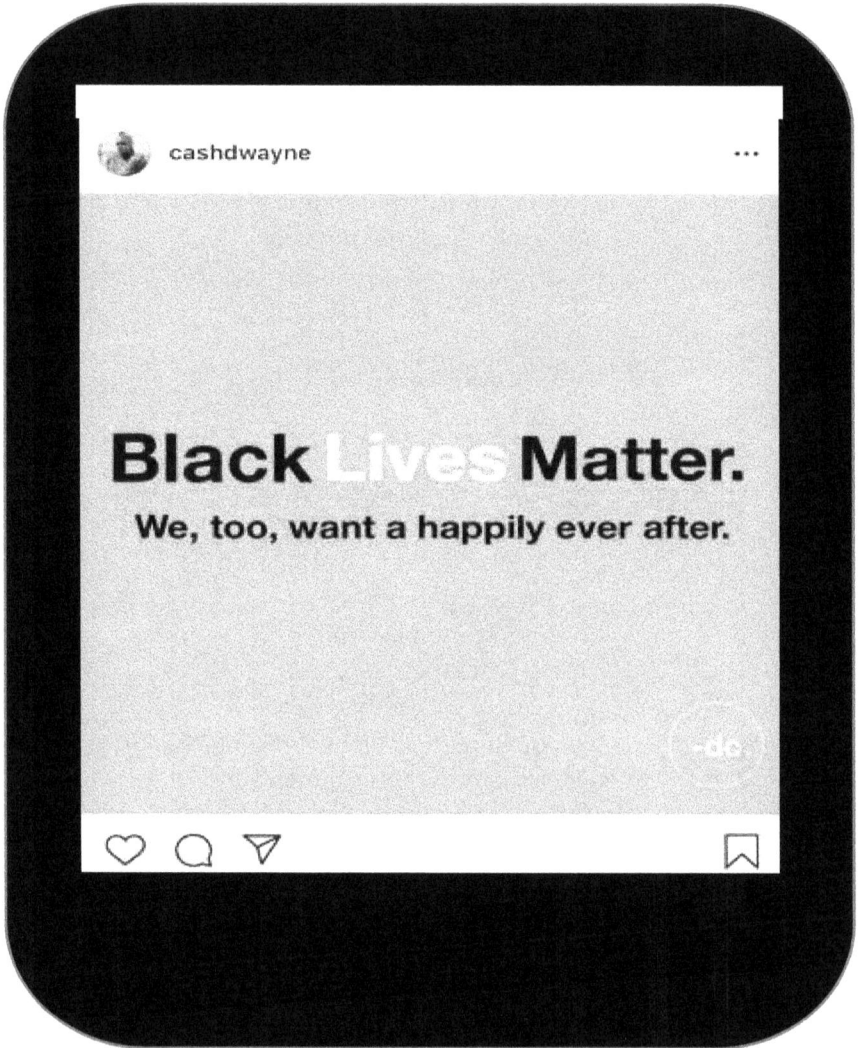

20

My Black Defined

Vonice Waynette

My black is embracing and loving everything my melanin has to offer.

From my textured hair to the fullness of my lips,

Rocking cornrows and shades, braids dripped in beads, shells and thangs,

Knowing that the world sees my being as a trending thing,

But understanding my black is more than a hashtag that causes other shades fame.

My black is nurturing to the soul and elevating to the spirit,

Walking this world unapologetic and living what our ancestors envisioned.

It's like taking a sip of black tea bold, strong and refreshing,

They try to deny, define and contain put us in a box and stand on it,

Not realizing that when they open their eyes we are uniquely undefined.

Inspiring the elevation of mental empowerment,

They can't figure out our expressive ways so they throw shame on it,

But then the beauty on the inside exudes the resilience to see it through,

We are far more than the school's history books laid out for you.

My black is knowing there are no levels to this because the sky is the limit,

The brilliance that encompasses my mind is irreplaceable and timeless,

We don't just break down barriers, we move mountains.

The pure embodiment of God's gifts and blessings divinely in alignment,

Humble yet powerful,

Youthful but seeks wisdom,

Our greatness is undeniable, phenomenal and real

To be connected to US is truly a big deal,

My. Black. Is.

Untitled

Lynesha Littleton   L♥E

Officer did you hear me?!?
Nah fam!
Probably cause I can't breathe
As you bend the knee
Using OUR protest against me
While no system of justice can defend me
Well... it can but it won't
"Don't let them stand, watch them choke"
"Have little Brad go start shit so they get riled up and
we say we were provoked"
Taking our voice as a joke
Filling the streets we walk with smoke
Yet forcing us to vote
Because hey, the better of the worse leaves us a little
less hurt?
We'd get to put in a little less work?
Before they ever give us freedom they're determined
to give us Death first!
"GET THEM OUTTA HERE, Let's see how these
bones in their necks work!"
"Shoot him a few times and let's just claim that he
reached for ..."
"Better yet we feared for our lives, this one unarmed
man and us four in our Teflon!"
This system is too far gone.

24

Treat them as they treat us is how change shall
come?!?
Eye for an eye because my cheeks all Gone!
Nowhere left to turn, white sheets all On
Disguised in blue suits but trust those white sheets are
at home.
I'm tired
But I'm not weak
We have a voice
We will speak
We have children
We will teach
We have US in Blue too, so Higher
We will reach!
While y'all laugh
We strategize
Y'all are awakening something DIVINE.
And together, our powers?!? Even you can't
DIVIDE!

Untitled Saida LeeKong

We say black lives matter
We wear it across our chest
to explain to the man with the bullet proof vest
that we are not a threat.

We are not animals, we deserve civil rights too, but
who exactly are we trying to prove our humanity to?
Over a hundred years ago Sojourner Truth said "but
ain't I a woman too?"
But that was hijacked by white women, now they call
it "me too".

They stole an entire country
we built the country but can't get 40 acres and a mule.
Y'all posting -we ain't our ancestors.
Yeah, don't be a bunch of fools. Our ancestors didn't
choose slavery. What's our excuse?
Now it's black children that knot their own noose.

We bought the American dream so bad but forgot we
are African American. We fight to be in their board
rooms and for them to tell us thanks for sharing. It's
not our humanity that needs to be explained, maybe
it's theirs?

26

We can't ask them to support the movement, when
they are the cause.
The definition of insanity is doing the same thing
expecting new results.
Well to be black in America is the definition of
insane.
To live with a double consciousness is not healthy for
the fittest of brains.

We have peacefully protested,
we have danced and sang begging for their acceptance
while killing our brothers cause they in the wrong
gang.

The war is on the home front. The enemy is within.
They let the chains go, but we lost ourselves.
The question isn't, does black life matter?
 of course it does!
But to who?
Does it need to matter to them or to you?

On being BLACK in the workplace.
Shelley Tyler Smith

Press through
Smile
Be your best self

Watch while
mediocrity is celebrated
because it

lacks Melanin

Melanin that makes up the composition
Of greatness, strength, resilience, brilliance,
resourcefulness

Magic....

Press through
Smile
Be your best self

So tired

But.............
Third verse same as the first.

28

2020 was like "Oh y'all want perfect vision? I got you."

Then it put a spotlight on:

· inequality
· racism
· the lack of
 preparedness for a pandemic
· toxic politics
· the dire need for healthcare in low income neighborhoods
· the trauma of being Black

Can y'all see now?

-dc

The Black Rule

Angel Blair

Growing up I was taught the golden rule - treat others
the way you want to be treated
Some were taught the black rule - to oppress others
until they feel defeated

How do I convince the black men in my life that who
they are matters and they're uniquely beautiful
Better yet, WHY do I have to convince them of
something this basic that is already truthful

The core of our being will always be overshadowed
by the skin that conceals it
Hidden racists wait for an opportune moment and
our black skin reveals it

No regard for our lives as if our hearts don't pump
and we don't breathe the same air
As if we aren't kings and queens continuously
kingdom building for our heirs

With tears in our eyes we mourn the losses of our
brothers and sisters over and over
With broken hearts and justifications for wrongful
actions that never provide closure

We, black people, are exhausted, yet too tired of the
double standard to sleep
How can we get adequate rest knowing that the seed
they sow, justice never reaps?

America, we need you to willingly open your heart,
speak up, and stop turning a blind eye
Display some empathy and don't let the black rule be
justification when another black man dies

Co-Vid:
A
parallel life form
exercising
it's right to live
by
taking
my breath away
I
Can't
Breathe

E.E. Pritchett

I CAN'T BREATHE Darnell Serrette

Yes Injustice is a Flaw...
And Yes Injustice is what we all saw...
May 25th 2020 witnessing this murder ... excuse me
execution... is the same execution we witnessed for
hundreds of years by America's paw....
PAW meaning Power Above Worth...
George Floyd only cried out what every Black
American has felt since birth...

I Can't Breathe...umbilical cord wrapped around my
neck... I Can't Breathe ... a noose wrapped around my
neck ..... I Can't Breathe...a knee on my neck ..I Can't
Breathe......

Yet you ignore my cry ... you ignored my cry .... you
ignore our sigh of rage and exhaustion...
The two mix as well as water and oil...
Cities go up in flames and precincts to a boil...

I Can't Breathe.......as I'm deceived to believe that I
have a chance ..... I can't breathe as I wear this thick
mask to evade this poison you call COVID....
Continuous Oppression Vanquished In Demise...
This mask I have never taken off ...this mask you just
couldn't see but has been there.. this mask I can't
remove because of fear...

Our 6 foot distance is you on top and me in the ground... I Can't Breathe .... not even a sound... I Can't Breathe...blood dripping from my nose to the ground... I Can't Breathe ... and all this because I'm brown.....I can't brrrree....

06.02.20
Shelley Tyler Smith

We got up this morning and decided
that we needed to take control of the day
So....
We packed a small bag and agreed to drive
3 hours
towards the ocean....

Before we drove off
we prayed...

For safety
to not be sought out
to walk in peace
to laugh in peace
to stand in the sand and marvel at the ocean
in peace....

*"Heavenly Father, we just want to make it to the ocean
without dying from racism."*

Funny that white couples don't have to pray that
prayer

So we drove....
and we made it to the ocean

with our small bag
and laughed, and slept, and sang
for a few hours
in peace....
And before we drove back home, we stood on the
sand and marveled at the ocean
and raised our fist to the sky
and prayed again

*"Heavenly Father, we just want to make it back home without
dying from racism"*

Funny that white couples don't have to pray that
same prayer
and I don't understand why?
because
Black Love Matters....

Personal Prose

Jo Ann Del Sardo

As I watch the racial revolution unfolding, I cannot

help but think about the late 60's and my own experiences as a protester. We knew back then that it was more than the Vietnam War that was at stake, social justice and Civil Rights were also a part of what we addressed. We could not separate one from the other. So, I watch the current protests address the same issues. It is heartening to see how this coalition is more diverse (I think of Jesse Jackson's Rainbow Coalition) and more energetic than we were. They are also much more knowledgeable than we were.

I get angry when I hear about things in American history that I was not aware of—feeling that if we knew we could have done something. I didn't know about Rosewood. I feel again that I have been lied to—through omission—hiding our history. I can't imagine how Black people in this country feel about that.

I have thought often about how Black people have managed to live in this country and maintain their faith. There have been many times that I have been lifted by that faith. I reflect on the young Black woman who said that we are lucky that Black people want equality and not revenge. And I wonder why. My friend helped me understand that the Black culture is rooted in Faith and again I am lifted up.

37

This time is different. I began feeling in the beginning of 2020 that something was in the air—not sure what it would be; but knowing that something had to give. Then after experiencing the Democratic Primaries I began to believe that something definitely was changing. I did not expect the pandemic to be as powerful as it has been.

Then the killing of George Floyd—in the midst of all of this- we witnessed his murder in front of our eyes and the country and then the world reacted. Would it have happened without the pandemic? Who knows, but something bigger than us is at work here, that I am sure of.

For me the protesters are light workers on the planet. They are changing the consciousness of our planet and people are responding. People that one would not expect to speak out so frankly and candidly. Police Chiefs, politicians, and others who usually side with the police have been so verbal and have taken part in the protests. They are bringing light to the dark places in our country and on the planet.

I think that there is a connection to the pandemic and the protests. Only light heals—and the pandemic is definitely a dark force. When we shed light on dark places, we must see it in full—

so the pandemic will get worse before it gets better, but I do believe that if we did not have these protests that are shedding light on so many issues, the pandemic would be even worse.

To Paul Laurence Dunbar,
with love, from 2020

Niambi LeeKong McLaurin

We wear our masks as we release the lies,
That hid their sins and shaded eyes,—
We have paid the debt of human guile;
With torn and bleeding hearts the earth we rile,

The world must now be over-wise,
We will make them count our tears and sighs!
Let them feel the truth-not hide
While we wear the mask.

Hidden smiles, and O great Christ, our cries
will break the chains and let tortured souls arise.
Beneath our feet, we march the miles;
To let the world wake from dreaming otherwise,
Because we wore the mask.

Paul Laurence Dunbar (1872-1906) was one of the first Black Poets to gain national recognition. The son of freed slaves, he wrote the famous poem *We Wear the Mask*.

Hey Google
Play "A change is gonna come"
by Sam Cooke.

And blast that sh*t.

-dc

Editor

Niambi L. McLaurin

Dwayne Cash

Shelley Tyler Smith

E.E. Pritchett

Rashaad Kareem

H. Saida LeeKong

Robertson Greene

Holly E. Chesnut

Dorissa Suttner

Jo Ann DeSanto

Lynesha Littleton

Angel Blair

Danielle Gilmore

Darnell Senette

Contributors

www.ingramcontent.com/pod-product-compliance
Lightning Source LLC
Chambersburg PA
CBHW060545030426
42337CB00021B/4435